WET CEMENT:

A MIX OF CONCRETE POEMS

Bob Raczka

ROARING BROOK PRESS
NEW YORK

ALSO BY BOB RACZKA

LEMONADE:
AND OTHER
POEMS
SQUEEZED FROM
A SINGLE
WORD

PRESIDENTIAL
MISADVENTURES:
POEMS THAT POKE FUN AT
THE MAN IN CHARGE

TABLE OF CONTENTS

word pa ntings

I like to think of poems as word paintings. A poet uses words like colors to paint pictures inside your head.

In concrete poems, or shape poems, the words also paint pictures on the page. The poet arranges words in the shape of the thing the poem is about or in a way that emphasizes the poem's meaning.

But here's what's really cool: by cleverly arranging individual letters, you can also paint a picture on the page with a single word. In this case, the letters become your colors.

In this book, I've done both. In the title of each poem, I've created pictures with letters. In the poems themselves, I've created pictures with words.

I hope these poems make you smile. I hope they make you look at words in a fresh way. Most of all, I hope they make you want to play with words yourself.

—Bob Raczka

Wright on course, headed for heaven. One two three four five six seven

akeoff

eight nine ten eleven twelve. Wright back down, but proud of himself.

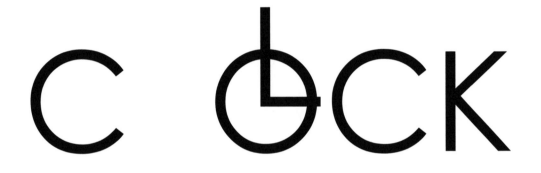

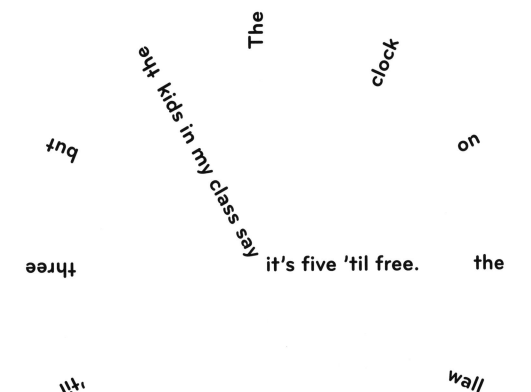

The clock on the wall says it's five 'til three, but kids in my class say it's five 'til free.

it's five 'til free.

BLUE SKY?

high

to   the

way

hop   our

could

if   we

What

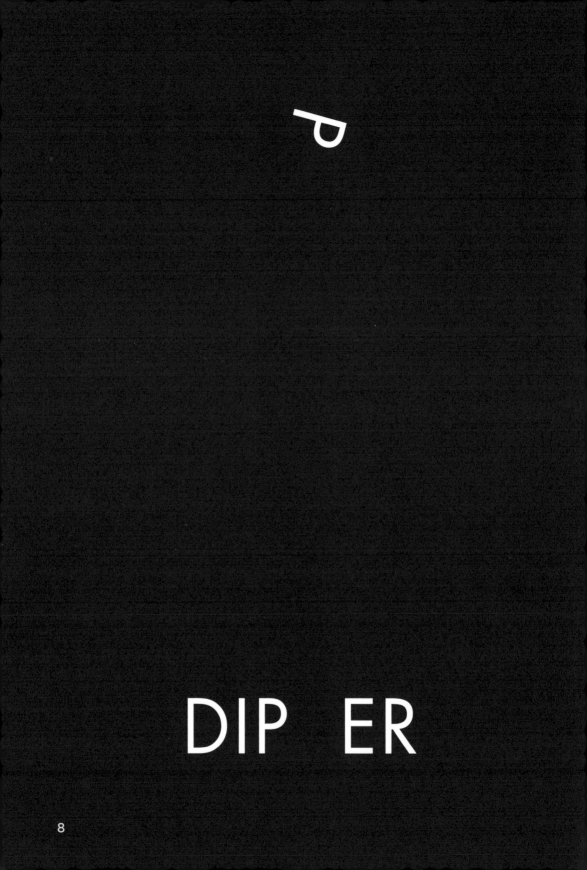

P

DIP ER

Way down there on earth you hold firefly jars, filled up to their lids with light. Up here in the sky, I'm a vessel of stars, my brim overflowing with night.

CROSS WORD

```
D
O
W
N         Y               S
O       ONLYDIRECTIONS
N         U               A
ACROSSARE                 L
N                         W
D                I        A
                 N        Y
        LOOKBOTHWAYSAT
                 E
                 R
                 S
                 E
                 C
                 T
                 I
                 O
                 N
                 S
```

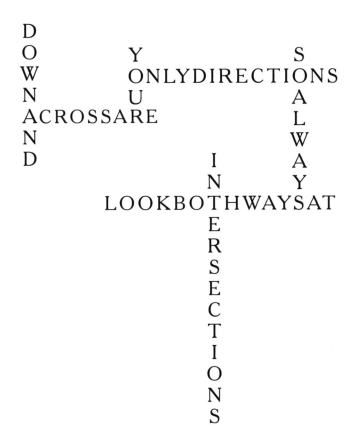

I hang out in blue jeans and comfy old shirts. I hang out in blouses and long frilly skirts. I hang out in sport coats and sweaters and shawls. I even hang out with no clothes on at all!

DOMINOES

JUST ONE PUSH HERE WE GO FOLLOW THROUGH FEEL THE FLOW BRACE YOURSELF STAY IN LINE STEADY NOW DOING FINE FORWARD MARCH DON'T LOOK BACK CAN'T STOP NOW STILL ON TRACK

COMING DOWN
SINGLE FILE
DO YOUR PART
JOIN THE PILE
TAG YOU'RE IT
FALLING FAST
PASS IT ON
WHAT A BLAST!
LOOKING GOOD
ALMOST THERE
STAY ON COURSE
DON'T BE SCARED
HANG ON TIGHT
ROCK 'N' ROLL
WHAT ARE WE?
DOMINOES!

XYLO
PHO
NE

It's really not a phone at all. It will not let me make a call.

It has no way to text or send an email to my web-

based friends. It doesn't have an app for

games. I really think it's been mis-

named. I will say one thing

for this phone. It has

unlimited ring

tones.

o

p p-up

Ball

Ball

Ball

Ball

Ball

I'm under it! I'm under it! I'm under it! I Ball blundered it.

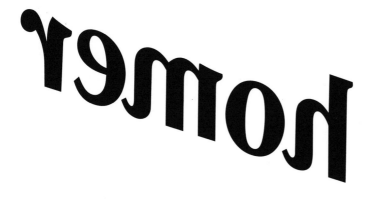

The pitcher hurls his hummer toward the slugger squeezing lumber CRACk! the slugger slams the hummer toward the bleachers for a homer.

here

I'm

I'm

there

I'm

near

·

firefly

far

I'm

you

try

to

catch

me

in

a

jar.

rbiti
ou
gu

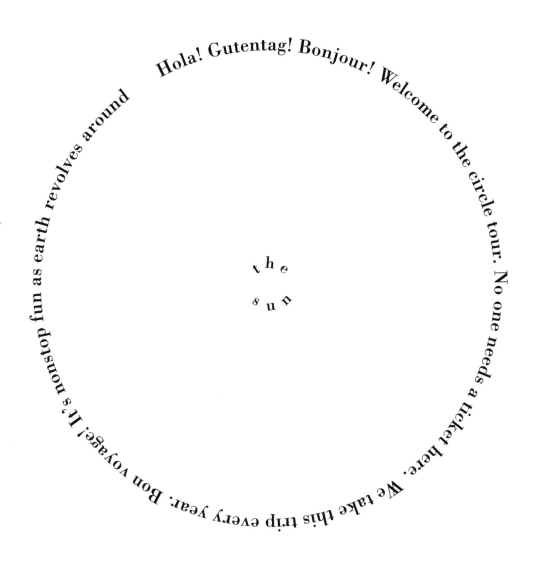

Hola! Gutentag! Bonjour! Welcome to the circle tour. No one needs a ticket here. We take this trip every year. Bon voyage! It's nonstop fun as earth revolves around the sun

CORNERS

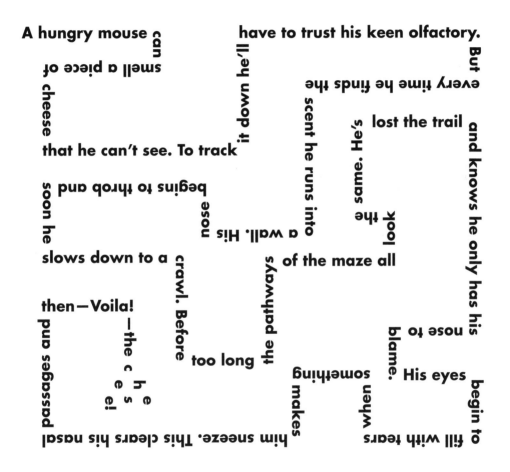

A hungry mouse can smell a piece of cheese that he can't see. To track it down he'll have to trust his keen olfactory. But every time he finds the scent he runs into a wall. His nose begins to throb and soon he slows down to a crawl. Before too long the pathways of the maze all look the same. He's lost the trail and knows he only has his nose to blame. His eyes begin to fill with tears when something makes him sneeze. This clears his nasal passages and then—Voila!—the cheese!

eracer

ERASERS WILL STICK BY YOU,
ON THAT YOU CAN DEPEND,
FORGIVING ALL YOUR DUMB MISSTAKES—

A FRIEND RIGHT TO THE END.

Holding their gold until November, our sugar maples will be the last trees to spend their

b
eau
ty

autum

u

Let them cool
overnight, then in the morning,

w a r m .

Careful not to
pick them 'til they're
long and clear and ripe.
Break one off and take a lick,
or if you're brave,
a bite!

Cold and smooth
and crunchy too, with just a
hint of sweet.
Mother Nature's
freeze pops,
the perfect winter t r e a t .

ICICles

When the snow

begins to melt and gutters

start to d r i p ,

frozen water harvesters

begin to

lick their lips.

Mother nature's recipe

is simple

as you please:

Let the snowflakes t h a w ,

then cook

at 32 degrees.

Thaw and cook

repeatedly until stalac t i t e s

form.

TUNNELS

Beneath the streets
        two
                stories
                        down
                                below
                                        the
                                                ground
                                                        the
                                                                subway
                                                                        rolls,

                                                A CITIFIED-

JUST-SLIDE-INSIDE-AND-TAKE-A-RIDE ELECTRIC MOLE.

GHTNING

from a bad mood sky,
tears,
then a jag-
ged
slash-
ing flash of anger,
ear-
splitting,
obnoxious,
a cloud tantrum

sunset

sunrise

breakfast

math quiz

noon

school's out

homework

sunset

moon

bal on

When
it first slipped out
of my hand, I was sad
to see my balloon floating
away, but as it rose higher
in the sky, I imagined it lan-
ding in some faraway yard,
where a kid like me would
find it and wonder how
far the balloon had
flown and who
held it
last,
and that thought made me smile.

poeTRY

poetry is about taking away the words you don't need

poetry is taking away words you don't need

poetry is words you need

poetry is words

try

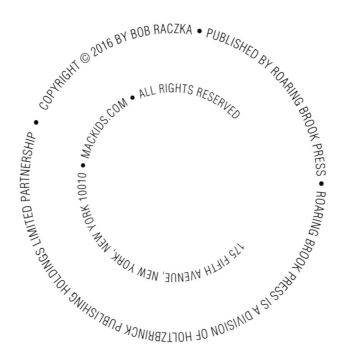
Library of Congress Cataloging-in-Publication Data

Names: Raczka, Bob, author.
Title: Wet cement : a mix of concrete poems / Bob Raczka.
Description: First edition. I New York : Roaring Brook Press, 2016.
Identifiers: LCCN 2015027142I ISBN 9781626722361 (hardcover) I ISBN 9781626722378 (ebook)
Subjects: I BISAC: JUVENILE NONFICTION / Poetry / General.
Classification: LCC PS3618.A346 A6 2016 I DDC 811/.6—dc23
LC record available at http://lccn.loc.gov/2015027142

Our books may be purchased in bulk for promotional, educational, or business use.
Please contact your local bookseller or the Macmillan Corporate and Premium Sales Department
at (800) 221-7945 ext. 5442 or by e-mail at MacmillanSpecialMarkets@macmillan.com.

First edition 2016
Book design by Kimi Weart
Printed in China by RR Donnelley Asia Printing Solutions Ltd., Dongguan City, Guangdong Province

5   7   9   10   8   6